games handbook

OUTDOOR GAMES!

Lisa Regan

QEB Publishing

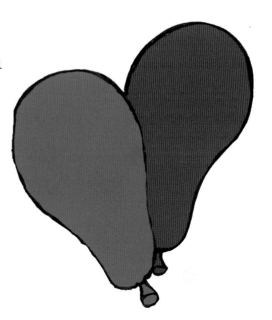

FX:11-14

Editor: Sarah Eason
Designer: Calcium
Illustrators: Owen Rimington and Emma DeBanks

Published in the United States by
QEB Publishing, Inc.
3 Wrigley, Suite A
Irvine, CA 92618

www.qed-publishing.co.uk

Library of Congress Cataloging-in-Publication Data

Regan, Lisa, 1971-
  Outdoor games / Lisa Regan.
     p. cm. -- (QEB games handbook)
  ISBN 978-1-59566-934-6 (library binding)
  1. Outdoor games--Juvenile literature. I. Title.
  GV1203.R44 2011
  790.192'2--dc22
                                2010014187

ISBN 978 1 59566 934 6

Printed in China

CONTENTS

HOW TO USE THIS BOOK

Let's play outside—here comes the sun! It's the perfect place to have some fun!

So, you are outside with space to run and to play whatever you like. Whether you are in the park, at the beach, in your own backyard or even in the school playground, there are some great games here to try. Make the most of running free and getting some fresh air and exercise—it's playtime!

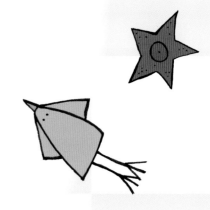

You will need

Many of the games in this book just need you and a few friends. Some of them need a ball, and a few suggest you use beach toys, yard toys or things you find around you, such as sticks and stones. There are also rules for games with special equipment, such as marbles—read through the book and take your pick.

Players

Lots of outdoor games were invented in the playground, where you have a big group of friends to play with. Some of the games in this book are good fun for a small group of players. If no one wants to play, read the "On your own?" feature to see how to adapt the game to play by yourself.

4

Difficulty

No one wants to waste time playing outdoor games with lots of complicated rules, so all these games are fairly easy. You will need to practice some games before you get really good at them. The easiest games are marked with * and are at the beginning of the book. The hardest games are at the end, marked * * * * *, and the games in between are—well, in between!

STEPPING STONES

Carefully move your box each time,
And head straight for the finish line.

Difficulty: ⭐⭐⭐ **Players:** 2 or more

You will need:
• two shoe boxes per player

1 This is a racing game. Play against the other players, or make two teams for a relay race.

2 Use your boxes as stepping stones. Put the first one down (with the open side facing up) and step into it. Put the second box in front and place your other foot inside.

3 Lift your back foot and move the empty box forward. Keep going until you reach the end. If it's a relay race, run back to the start and pass the boxes to the next player.

On Your Own?
Use a stopwatch to record how fast you can race from one end of the garden to the other.

Bet You Can't!
Make a rule that you must return to the start if your foot touches the ground.

The winner is...
the first team or person to reach the finish line—without collapsing in a heap or breaking their boxes!

20

RIVER MONSTER

Aagh! Don't let the monster get you,
But cross the river if it lets you.

Difficulty: ⭐⭐⭐ **Players:** 3 or more

You will need:
• skipping rope or string

1 Mark out the banks of a "river" using jump ropes, string, or lines drawn in the sand.

2 Two players stand in the river and form the "monster" by linking arms. The other players have to run across the river as the monster tries to catch them.

3 Anyone who is caught joins arms and makes the monster longer. The monster cannot let any part of its body go out of the river. It becomes harder to get away as the monster grows longer!

The winner is...
the last person who hasn't been caught.

On Your Own?
Mark out the riverbanks and see if you can leap across without "falling in." How far can you leap?

Did You Know?
Don't try to play this game on the Amazon River in South America. Where it flows through Brazil, it is between 4 and 6 mi (6 and 10 km) wide!

21

Bet You Can't!

Are you too good already? Beaten all your friends and smashed the world record? Then read this section for an extra challenging twist to put your skills to the test. Now let's see how good you are!

Did You Know?

For some games you will find fascinating facts related to them, to add to the fun.

BALLOON BASH

Throw your balloons up into the air.
Hit them, though you can't see where!

Difficulty: **Players:** 2 or more

You will need:
- balloons
- scarf
- tennis racket or newspaper

1 Take turns covering your eyes with a scarf (carefully), so that you cannot see the balloons. The other players can stop you from tripping or bumping into things.

2 Throw the balloons gently up into the air. Use a tennis racket or a rolled-up newspaper to try to hit a balloon.

3 Score a point for every time you make a hit. You'll be able to feel it, and the non-blindfolded players can keep count as well.

On Your Own?
Use a long piece of string to tie a balloon to a tree or fence, and hit the balloon by yourself. If you don't move too far, you won't hurt yourself.

The winner is... the first to get 10 points.

STOMP!

Jump around and stamp and hop—
Just don't let your balloon go pop!

Difficulty: **Players:** any number

3 Make sure you keep an eye on your own balloon—others will be out to get it!

The winner is...
the last person left with an unbroken balloon.

1 Tie a balloon to the ankle of each player. Use up to a yard of thread for each one, so the balloons float away a little.

2 When someone says, "Go!" you must run and jump around, trying to burst the other players' balloons.

Did You Know?
Don't play this game with British TV star Dermot O'Leary. In 2008, he held the world "balloon popping" record—he burst 100 balloons in 25 seconds!

On Your Own?
Use a longer piece of string and run around in all directions, trying to jump on your own balloon!

TREASURE HUNT

**Treasures are waiting to be found—
Where can they be? Just look around!**

Difficulty: ⭐ **Players:** any number

You will need:
....
• small box such as a matchbox

3 Keep checking to make sure your box closes with all your things in it. Do not pick flowers or pick up litter. Do not disturb animal homes, such as birds' nests.

1 This game is easy, and can take as long as you like. Start by giving each player a small empty box.

2 Hunt around your outdoor space looking out for tiny things. The aim is to put as many different items into your box as possible.

The winner is...
the person who collects the greatest number of different things.

On Your Own?
This is loads of fun for one player—but don't wander off too far from a grown-up.

Bet You Can't!
List three items that everyone HAS to find, such as a petal, a blade of grass, and a wood chip.

POOH STICKS

**Throw your stick and watch it flow—
Gently as the water flows.**

Difficulty: **Players:** 2 or more

Don't play this game without having an adult there to supervise you.

1 You have to play this game standing on a bridge over a stream. Be careful! Make sure you stand upstream, so the water is flowing under the bridge behind you.

2 Each player chooses a stick. Try to pick one that looks different from the others, so that you can tell which one is yours.

3 Drop all the sticks into the stream all at the same time, then run to the other side of the bridge, and wait...

Did You Know?
This game is named after Winnie the Pooh, the bear who plays it with Christopher Robin in the stories by A.A. Milne.

The winner is...
the person whose stick appears first from under the bridge.

STAR WARS

Don't step on cracks seen in the street. This game is best if you have small feet!

Difficulty: **Players:** any number

1 Here's a game to play walking down the street. It's fun on a long shopping trip.

On Your Own?

This is really easy to play alone—but harder if you are in a hurry!

2 As you walk along the sidewalk, try not to step on the cracks between the paving slab.

3 Carefully place your feet so they are totally inside each paving slab. Anyone who steps on a crack goes over to the Dark Side of the Force!

Bet You Can't!

See if you are skilled enough to play on tiny slabs. You have to tiptoe! That's why Darth Vader is on the dark side—his feet are too big!

The winner is...

anyone who stays off all the cracks. You can play with grown-ups, even if they don't know they are playing!

You will need:
....
• just your feet!

GIANT'S SHOES

**Fee-fi-fo-fum,
Who'll be the fastest in this run?**

Difficulty: ⭐⭐ **Players:** 2 players or 2 equal teams

You will need:
....
- two pairs of BIG shoes
- jump rope or string
- chalk

3 If you are playing in teams, take off the shoes so that the next team member can race in them.

1 Make a starting line and a finish line. Use jump ropes or string, or draw a line with chalk. Put a pair of giant shoes on the starting line for each player or team.

2 When someone says, "Go!" players put on the shoes and carefully race toward the finish line, then turn around and run back to the starting line.

The winner is...

the person, or team, that finishes first. Anyone who loses a shoe must put it on again before they can continue running.

On Your Own?

Make an obstacle course and run around it wearing your giant's shoes.

Bet You Can't!

Make the game harder by running sideways, or even backward. If you're just too good for this game, turn it into an egg and spoon race using rubber balls and spoons.

11

MR. WOLF

**Slowly creep up to the line,
But run when Wolf shouts, "Dinnertime!"**

Difficulty: ⭐⭐ **Players:** any number

You will need:
·····················
- large space

1 Choose one player to be Mr. Wolf. He stands a few yards away from the others, with his back turned. The players stand in a row and shout, "What time is it, Mr. Wolf?"

3 If Mr. Wolf shouts "Dinner time!" or if a player gets near enough to touch Mr Wolf. he chases everyone back to the starting line.

2 Mr. Wolf answers, "Three o'clock!" and the players creep forward three steps. Each time they ask, he can say a different time, and they move that number of steps. If Mr. Wolf turns around, the players must freeze.

Bet You Can't!
Make the game more fun on a hot day by giving Mr. Wolf a watering can. Anyone he catches gets sprinkled!

The winner is...
anyone who gets back to the start without being caught. If Mr Wolf catches someone, they become Mr. Wolf.

On Your Own?
Practice creeping up on a chosen place, such as a tree—if you hear a noise, such as a siren, a bus, or even birdsong, you must freeze.

12

SPLASH!

**Play this on a sunny day
To wash your cobwebs clean away!**

Difficulty: ⭐⭐ **Players:** 2 or more

You will need:
....
- water bomb balloons

1 This game is very easy, but SO splashy! Fill a water bomb balloon so that it is pretty full, and tie the end.

2 Throw the water bomb from player to player. Be careful not to drop it, or you'll get wet!

3 Be careful, too, how you catch it. It's easy to burst a water bomb just by closing your hands around it!

Bet You Can't!
Play over a clothes line or tennis net. The throws will have to be bold, so everyone will have to be on their guard!

On Your Own?
See how brave you can be—throw the water bomb higher each time, and make sure you catch it!

The winner is...
there is no winner —just a lot of wet players, usually!

FINDERS KEEPERS

Play this game of treasure seekers.
Look for money—finders keepers!

Difficulty: ⭐⭐ **Players:** any number

You will need:
• pencils
• paper
• coins

1 Each player writes a list of things to find. It can include nature items (such as leaves or seeds) or toys, but not pieces of litter. The choice will depend of whether you are at the park, in the backyard or at the beach.

2 Exchange lists with another player. Set a time limit for each player to collect as many listed items as they can.

3 For an added bonus, write "coin" on the lists and ask a grown-up to hide small change nearby.

The winner is... the person who collects the most things on their list. Remember not to stray too far.

On Your Own? Find your own things, or ask a grown-up to make a list for you.

Did You Know? Dandelions get their name from the French *dent de lion*, which means "lion's tooth."

CRAZY GOLF

Crazy golf is so much fun—
Can you score a hole in one?

Difficulty: ⭐⭐ **Players:** any number

3 Use a ball and a stick, or a mini golf set, to play around the course.

1 Set up your own crazy golf course, using anything you can find as obstacles. If you are at the beach, dig holes in the sand and build walls and tunnels.

2 If you are in the backyard, use flowerpots on their side for the holes, and make a course with the garden hose, around a swing, under a bench... make it as difficult as you like.

The winner is...
the person who takes the fewest shots to finish—but half the fun is setting up the crazy course!

On Your Own?

No problem—you can play this by yourself for hours.

Did You Know?

Mini golf is played semiprofessionally by some people. There are mini golf tournaments, where it is possible to win up to $5,000 as prize money, so start practicing!

15

WORKS OF ART

Pile your stones up, nice and tall.
Make sure you don't let them fall!

Difficulty: **Players:** any number

You will need:
• pebbles
• stones
• rocks

1 Each player collects a heap of pebbles, stones, and small rocks. Find a flat surface to work on.

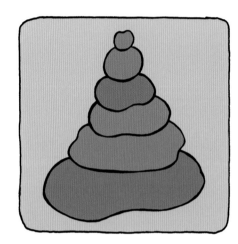

3 Experiment with different designs, or just try to make the tallest tower you can!

On Your Own?
This game is a great way to pass time alone, and you can really concentrate on what you're doing.

2 The idea is simple—pile up the stones, starting with the largest at the bottom, to make a sculpture.

The winner is...
the person with the tallest sculpture, or the most artistic, or the best balanced... you decide.

Did You Know?
Rock balancing is recognized as art, and has been made famous by artists such as Bill Dan in the US and Andy Goldsworthy in Britain.

16

OLYMPIC RINGS

Do your friends say you're acting loopy? Tell them you're just hula hoopy!

Difficulty: ⭐⭐ **Players:** any number

1 There are lots of games to play with rings and hoops. Try standing a few yards away from a target, such as a bucket or a small chair. See if you can throw your hoop so it lands over the target.

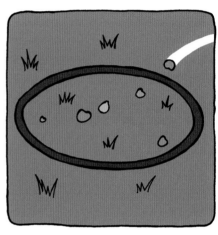

2 Hoop rolling is harder than it looks. Can you roll your hoop, on its side, so that it goes between two goalposts?

3 Place the hoop on the ground and stand a few yards back. Try to throw stones or balls so they land inside the hoop, without touching the edges.

Did You Know?

Historians have found that people played games with hoops (made of woven grass or sticks) thousands of years ago in ancient Egypt.

On Your Own?

No problem—practice all the events alone and try to beat your own best scores.

The winner is...
the person who wins the most events in your own hula Olympics.

FROG HOPPERS

You will need:
....
- newspaper

**Leap onto a lily pad
To make that heron hopping mad!**

Difficulty: **Players:** the more the better

2 The players run around until a grown-up shouts out, "Here comes the heron!" Everyone has to hop onto a lily pad to stay safe.

3 When the grown-up says "Hmm, nothing to eat today," everyone runs around again. Take away one of the lily pads each time, so that it becomes harder to find a safe place.

1 Place single sheets of newspaper all around your playing area, but not touching each other. These are your "lily pads."

On Your Own?
Leap from one lily pad to another, making the gaps between them bigger each time.

The winner is...
the last "frog" on the last lily pad.

Did You Know?
The largest heron in the United States, the great blue heron, doesn't just eat frogs. It also gobbles down lizards, snakes, muskrats, prairie dogs, and baby alligators!

BOULES

Here's a game that takes some skill,
Winning gives you such a thrill!

Difficulty: ⭐⭐⭐ **Players:** 2 or more

You will need:
....
- one small ball or stone
- two bigger balls or stones per player

1 One player throws the small ball or stone across the play area. Try to throw it about 5 yards. This is the "jack."

2 Each player throws their first ball or stone, trying to make it land as close to the jack as possible. If you are using stones, choose ones that are different from each other so you can tell which are yours.

3 The players then take their second throw. Aim to land closest to the jack, or to knock any of the other balls or stones out of the way.

On Your Own?

This game is addictive, and you can spend ages practicing on your own to get really good.

Bet You Can't!

Hit the jack and knock it out of the way of the other players' balls.

The winner is...

the person whose ball or stone is closest to the jack.

STEPPING STONES

Carefully move your box each time,
And head straight for the finish line.

Difficulty: ⭐⭐⭐ **Players:** 2 or more

1 This is a racing game. Play against the other players, or make two teams for a relay race.

You will need:
....
- two shoe boxes per player

2 Use your boxes as stepping stones. Put the first one down (with the open side facing up) and step into it. Put the second box in front and place your other foot inside.

3 Lift your back foot and move the empty box forward. Keep going until you reach the end. If it's a relay race, run back to the start and pass the boxes to the next player.

On Your Own?

Use a stopwatch to record how fast you can race from one end of the garden to the other.

Bet You Can't!

Make a rule that you must return to the start if your foot touches the ground.

The winner is...

the first team or person to reach the finish line—without collapsing in a heap or breaking their boxes!

RIVER MONSTER

You will need:
....
• skipping rope or string

Aagh! Don't let the monster get you,
But cross the river if it lets you.

Difficulty: ⭐⭐⭐ **Players:** 3 or more

3 Anyone who is caught joins arms and makes the monster longer. The monster cannot let any part of its body go out of the river. It becomes harder to get away as the monster grows longer!

1 Mark out the banks of a "river" using jump ropes, string, or lines drawn in the sand.

2 Two players stand in the river and form the "monster" by linking arms. The other players have to run across the river as the monster tries to catch them.

The winner is...
the last person who hasn't been caught.

On Your Own?
Mark out the riverbanks and see if you can leap across without "falling in." How far can you leap?

Did You Know?
Don't try to play this game on the Amazon River in South America. Where it flows through Brazil, it is between 4 and 6 mi (6 and 10 km) wide!

IN THE MONEY

Water, water, everywhere.
If you win the money, will you share?

Difficulty: ⭐⭐⭐ **Players:** any number

You will need:
....
- large silver coin
- copper coins
- bucket of water

3 Try holding your copper coin higher or lower before you drop it. It is hard to hit the silver coin, because as the water makes the falling coins move in unexpected directions.

1 Put the large silver coin in the bucket of water, roughly in the middle.

2 Take turns dropping a copper coin into the water and see if it lands on, or partly on, the silver coin.

The winner is...
the person whose coin lands closest to the silver one. They might even get to keep it!

Did You Know?
In Russia in 1940, hundreds of coins fell from the sky one day. A money chest had been lifted up by a great wind called a tornado, and the coins fell out—as if someone in the heavens was playing this game!

On Your Own?
This game is just as frustrating when you play alone!

SILLY OLYMPICS

See if you can be the best.
Win your races—beat the rest.

Difficulty: ⭐⭐⭐ **Players:** any number

You will need:
....
• outdoor toys

1 Hold your own Olympic Games with a selection of zany races. Mark out a start and finish line, and decide how many events you want to include.

Bet You Can't!
Do the same races over a home-made obstacle course.

2 Try to vary the skills you need. Balancing events could be running while carrying a ball on a shovel (something like egg and spoon), keeping a balloon balanced on your forehead as you run, or crawling with a bucket of water on your back.

3 Silly running races could be running backward, a three-legged race, running with a ball held between your knees, or dribbling a balloon without letting it touch the ground.

On Your Own?
You might feel silly, but these games are great on your own.

The winner is... probably a little nutty and also out of breath!

OFF THE WALL

Throw your stone against a wall. The trick is where you make it fall.

Difficulty: ⭐⭐⭐ **Players:** any number

3 The aim is to get your stone to fall close to the wall, rather than bouncing back and landing far away. It's tricky!

1 Each player finds a pebble they can recognize as their own. Look for different colors and shapes.

2 Take turns throwing your pebble against the wall. It will bounce back and land on the ground (as stones do).

The winner is... the person whose stone is closest to the bottom of the wall.

Did You Know?
One of the world's biggest rocks is Uluru, in Australia. Don't try to play this game with it—it's over over 2,500 ft (800 m) high and nearly 6 mi (10 km) around its edge.

On Your Own?
You can spend ages perfecting your skill.

SHARPSHOOTERS

**Try to be the marble king
By knocking others from the ring.**

Difficulty: ⭐⭐⭐ **Players:** any number

1 Draw a large circle on the ground. Draw in the dirt or sand, or use chalk. Each player puts ten small marbles in the middle of the circle.

2 Standing about two feet away, take turns rolling or throwing a larger marble into the circle, aiming for the other marbles.

3 Score a point for any marbles that you knock outside the circle. If your large marble rolls out of the circle, you can take another turn where it landed.

Bet You Can't!
Sometimes this game is played "for keeps"—any marbles you knock out are yours to keep. Everyone must agree at the beginning that they want to play this way.

On Your Own?
Take three turns and add up your score. Can you beat it with another three turns?

The winner is...
the person who scores the most points.

SLAM!

**Show off your talent with a ball—
Do some tricks against the wall!**

Difficulty: ⭐⭐⭐⭐ **Players:** any number

You will need:
....
- ball (any kind)
- wall

3 Make it harder by trying some tricks— such as clapping, spinning around, or touching the ground— between throwing and catching the ball. You have to be quick!

1 Find a high wall, such as the side of a building. Stand a little way back, then throw the ball so that it bounces on the ground and then hits the wall.

2 As the ball comes back off the wall, try to catch it. Easy, right?

The winner is... the person who can do the best tricks.

Bet You Can't!
Touch the ground, do a jumping jack and clap behind your back before catching the ball.

On Your Own?
No problem. You can easily play by yourself and try harder tricks each time.

BEACH PARTY

**Wait until you hear your name,
Then run like crazy in this game!**

Difficulty: ⭐⭐⭐⭐ **Players:** as many as possible

2 Each player is named after an item found at the beach, such as a shell or a towel. One player makes up a story about a trip to the beach.

1 Players sit opposite each other, with their legs out straight and feet touching.

On Your Own?
Make up a story that includes all the things you can see around you at the beach.

3 If you hear your item mentioned in the story, you must stand up and race to the end of the row, stepping in between the legs. Then run back around the outside, and up through the middle, to sit in your place again.

Did You Know?
Sandwiches are not named after the sand you get in them at the beach. They are named after an Englishman, the Earl of Sandwich, who liked them because they were easy to eat without a knife and fork.

The winner is...
no one, but the game goes crazy when more than one player is racing around.

HOPSCOTCH

Throw your stone and take a leap.
Try not to end up in a heap!

Difficulty: ⭐⭐⭐⭐ **Players:** any number

You will need:
• stone
• chalk

1 Copy the picture here to make a hopscotch board on the ground. Use chalk, or if you're at the beach, draw the lines and numbers in the sand.

2 Stand in front of the first square and throw the stone so that it lands in the number 1 square, without touching the sides.

3 Now for the hopping. Hop over square 1 into square 2, then square 3. Jump into 4 and 5 with one foot in each. Hop into 6, jump into 7 and 8, and then jump all the way around to face back toward the start.

Did You Know?

There is a French version of this game that is played on a spiral-shaped board. It is called *escargot* which means "snail," because of the shell shape of the court.

5 Now try to throw the stone into each of the other squares in turn. Repeat the hopping and jumping, so that you do not land on the square with the stone in it. Each time you return, bend down and pick up the stone.

6 If you fall, land on the square with the stone in it, or miss the square when you throw the stone, you are out and the next person has a turn. When it's your turn again, start with the square you missed on.

4 Hop and jump back to square 2. Bend over, balancing on one leg, and pick up the stone, then hop back to the start.

On Your Own?

Play in the same way, but if you miss go back to square 1 and start again.

The winner is...
anyone who goes through all the squares without a mistake.

PIRATE SHIP

Pretend you're on a pirate ship.
This fast-paced game will keep you fit.

Difficulty: ⭐⭐⭐⭐ **Players:** as many as possible

1 One person stands at the side and calls out the instructions. The other players start in the middle of the playing area.

2 As the caller shouts instructions, all the players must follow orders as quickly as possible—without making any mistakes.

3 The instructions all include an action—these are listed on the opposite page. Anyone who gets it wrong is out of the game. The caller can try to confuse everyone by shouting lots of instructions right after each other.

The winner is...
the last person standing!

Did You Know?
Pirates believed that whistling on board ship would cause a storm—so there is nothing in this game that mentions whistling!

Instructions

Port
Run to the left of the playing area.

Starboard
Run to the right of the playing area.

Bow of the ship
Run to the front of the playing area.

Stern of the ship
Run to the back of the playing area.

Scrub the decks
Kneel on the ground and pretend to clean it.

Captain's coming
Stand up straight and salute.

Man overboard
Put your hand above your eyes as if you are looking for something.

Climb the rigging
Move your arms and legs as if you're climbing a ladder.

Ship's cat
Meow and use your hand to wash your whiskers.

Storm at sea
Stagger backwards as if you are going to fall overboard.

On Your Own?
Act out your own pirate adventure, using these instructions and any other piratey things you can think of.

31

TWO BALL

So you think you're good at catch?
This game will show you've met your match.

Difficulty: **Players:** any number

1 This game is a bit like juggling, but you play against a wall. Throw your first ball so that it comes straight back at you without bouncing on the ground.

2 Before you catch the first ball, throw the second ball at the wall in the same way.

3 Catch the first ball and throw it straight back, in time to catch the second ball. Keep going!

On Your Own?
This game is just as good if you are the only player.

The winner is...
the player who keeps going the longest without dropping either ball.